Folk Dance

North American Folklore

Children's Folklore
Christmas and Santa Claus Folklore
Contemporary Folklore
Ethnic Folklore
Family Folklore
Firefighters' Folklore
Folk Arts and Crafts
Folk Customs
Folk Dance
Folk Fashion
Folk Festivals
Folk Games
Folk Medicine
Folk Music
Folk Proverbs and Riddles
Folk Religion
Folk Songs
Folk Speech
Folk Tales and Legends
Food Folklore
Regional Folklore

North American Folklore

Folk Dance

BY SHERRY BONNICE

Mason Crest Publishers

Mason Crest Publishers Inc.
370 Reed Road
Broomall, Pennsylvania 19008
(866) MCP-BOOK (toll free)
www.masoncrest.com

First printing
1 2 3 4 5 6 7 8 9 10
Library of Congress Cataloging-in-Publication Data on file at the Library of Congress.
ISBN 1-59084-337-1
       1-59084-328-2 (series)

Design by Lori Holland.
Composition by Bytheway Publishing Services, Binghamton, New York.
Cover design by Joe Gilmore.
Printed and bound in the Hashemite Kingdom of Jordan.

Picture credits:
Corel: pp. 6, 8, 10, 15, 17, 20, 22, 24, 26, 27, 29, 30, 32, 40, 42, 45, 52, 54, 57, 58, 59,
       60, 70, 72, 74, 75, 76, 79, 80, 84, 86, 88, 90, 93, 94, 95, 96, 98, 99, 100
PhotoAlto: p. 64
PhotoDisc: p. 62
Cover: "Dancing with Grandfather" by Charles A. MacLellan © 1914 SEPS: Licensed by
       Curtis Publishing, Indianapolis, IN. www.curtispublishing.com

Contents

Folklore grows from long-ago
seeds. Just as an acorn sends
down roots even as it shoots up
leaves across the sky, folklore is
rooted deeply in the past and
yet still lives and grows today.
It spreads through our modern
world with branches as wide
and sturdy as any oak's;
it grounds us in yesterday even
as it helps us make sense of
both the present and the future.

INTRODUCTION

by Dr. Alan Jabbour

WHAT DO A TALE, a joke, a fiddle tune, a quilt, a jig, a game of jacks, a saint's day procession, a snake fence, and a Halloween costume have in common? Not much, at first glance, but all these forms of human creativity are part of a zone of our cultural life and experience that we sometimes call "folklore."

The word "folklore" means the cultural traditions that are learned and passed along by ordinary people as part of the fabric of their lives and culture. Folklore may be passed along in verbal form, like the urban legend that we hear about from friends who assure us that it really happened to a friend of their cousin. Or it may be tunes or dance steps we pick up on the block, or ways of shaping things to use or admire out of materials readily available to us, like that quilt our aunt made. Often we acquire folklore without even fully realizing where or how we learned it.

Though we might imagine that the word "folklore" refers to cultural traditions from far away or long ago, we actually use and enjoy folklore as part of our own daily lives. It is often ordinary, yet we often remember and prize it because it seems somehow very special. Folklore is culture we share with others in our communities, and we build our identities through the sharing. Our first shared identity is family identity, and family folklore such as shared meals or prayers or songs helps us develop a sense of belonging. But as we grow older we learn to belong to other groups as well. Our identities may be ethnic, religious, occupational, or regional—or all of these, since no one has only one cultural identity. But in every case, the identity is anchored and strengthened by a variety of cultural traditions in which we participate and share with our neighbors. We feel the threads of connection with people we know, but the threads extend far beyond our own immediate communities. In a real sense, they connect us in one way or another to the world.

Folklore possesses features by which we distinguish ourselves from each other. A certain dance step may be African American, or a certain story urban, or a certain hymn Protestant, or a certain food preparation Cajun. Folklore can distinguish us, but at the same time it is one of the best ways we introduce ourselves to each other. We learn about new ethnic groups on the North American landscape by sampling their cuisine, and we enthusiastically adopt musical ideas from other communities. Stories, songs, and visual designs move from group to group, enriching all people in the process. Folklore thus is both a sign of identity, experienced as a special marker of our special groups, and at the same time a cultural coin that is well spent by sharing with others beyond our group boundaries.

Folklore is usually learned informally. Somebody, somewhere, taught us that jump rope rhyme we know, but we may have trouble remembering just where we got it, and it probably wasn't in a book that was assigned as homework. Our world has a domain of formal knowledge, but folklore is a domain of knowledge and culture that is learned by sharing and imitation rather than formal instruction. We can study it formally—that's what we are doing now!—but its natural arena is in the informal, person-to-person fabric of our lives.

Not all culture is folklore. Classical music, art sculpture, or great novels are forms of high art that may contain folklore but are not themselves folklore. Popular music or art may be built on folklore themes and traditions, but it addresses a much wider and more diverse audience than folk music or folk art. But even in the world of popular and mass culture, folklore keeps popping up around the margins. E-mail is not folklore—but an e-mail smile is. And college football is not folklore—but the wave we do at the stadium is.

This series of volumes explores the many faces of folklore throughout the North American continent. By illuminating the many aspects of folklore in our lives, we hope to help readers of the series to appreciate more fully the richness of the cultural fabric they either possess already or can easily encounter as they interact with their North American neighbors.

For Native Americans, dance is a part of their religious expression.

ONE

Folk Dance Across
North America

Light Feet and Joyful Hearts

Hawaiian girls identify with their cultural heritage with special dances and elaborate costumes.

ALONG TIME AGO, down south there lived a girl named Blanche, her sister Rose, and her mother. Blanche was a sweet, obedient child who did whatever she was told without complaining. Rose, however, was a complaining girl who sat around watching her sister work. The mother favored Rose because she was very much like her, and the two dreamed of someday leaving their run-down cabin for the city and all the finer things in life.

One day Rose and her mother sent Blanche to get cool water from the well. While there, Blanche met an old woman in a raggedy black shawl.

"Please give me some water from the well," she said to Blanche.

"Yes, ma'am," said Blanche as she dipped cool water from her bucket.

"Thank you, child. You have a giving spirit. God is going to bless you."

When Blanche returned home to her mother and sister, they were very angry. She had taken too long to get the water and they were so thirsty. Rose gulped down the water, and then they both began hitting the younger sister.

Frightened, Blanche ran into the woods crying. As she went along the path she met the old woman again.

"Why are you crying, child?" she asked.

When Blanche told of the beatings from her mother and her sister, the woman said she could come home with her—but she had to make one promise.

Traditional Hawaii folkdancers.

"You can't laugh at anything you see," the old woman said.

Blanched promised not to and they walked deeper into the woods. Soon they arrived at a very shabby cabin. In the front yard, a two-headed cow with corkscrew horns was capering and dancing. Blanche was very surprised at the sight.

Then she saw the chickens dancing around the cow's feet. They were all different colors and hopped on one, two, three feet and more. But as strange as it all was, Blanche kept her promise and did not even smile.

Inside the cabin, the old woman asked Blanche to cook dinner. From an old beef bone, Blanche made a bubbling stew and from a single grain of rice she had a bowl overflowing of tender rice.

After their meal, the old woman took Blanche outside onto the porch. Suddenly dozens of rabbits arrived in the yard, dressed in frock-coats and trail-train dresses. They danced on their hind feet. One rabbit played a banjo and they did a square dance, a Virginia Reel, and even a cakewalk. Blanche loved the danc-

Square dancing is the only four-couple dance set in a square whose steps are prompted by a caller. Some square dances have names like: "Texas Star," "Wagon Wheel," "Cumberland Gap," and "Cripple Creek."

John Griffin was a well-known itinerant dance master whose career has been documented by studying old newspaper notices and the dates inscribed in his dance manuals. He taught classes from Rhode Island and New Hampshire to as far south as South Carolina.

ing; her own feet twitched and her legs kicked, until finally she too was dancing. She danced all through the night, filled with a joy she had never known.

In the morning, when the old woman asked her to milk the cow, Blanche was still dancing. "You've got to go home now, child," the old woman told her. "But things will be different. And since you are such a good girl, I have a present for you.

"Go out into the chicken coop and take any eggs that say, 'Take me.' But be sure to leave the ones that say 'Don't take me.' On the way home throw the eggs over your left shoulder and you will see the surprise."

Blanche could not seem to stop her feet from dancing, but she went to the chicken coop and did exactly what she was told, even though the eggs that said "Don't take me' were beautiful golds and silvers, and the ones that said 'Take me' were just plain white.

Blanche danced all the way home, throwing the plain white eggs over her shoulder. They turned into wonderful things like gold and silver coins, a handsome carriage with a pony, silk and

satin dresses, and diamonds and rubies. Blanche loaded all the presents into the carriage and went home.

Her mother treated her much kinder. She even cooked dinner that night. But Blanche couldn't stop dancing.

While Blanche skipped and twirled in the moonlight, her mother and her sister decided that Rose would visit the old woman the next day to get more eggs, so they could move to the city forever.

Rose's visit was not like Blanche's, however. She laughed at the two-headed cow and the colored chickens. She complained about the beef-bone soup and she told the woman to give her the eggs too or she would hurt her. And she didn't have even the faintest urge to dance.

The old woman told Rose the same thing she had Blanche. "Take only the eggs that say 'Take me' and leave the ones that say 'Don't take me.'"

But Rose couldn't resist the gold and silver eggs, and when she threw them over her shoulder, wasps and wolves and other mean creature began to chase her. She trudged home with heavy feet. When she reached the cabin her mother tried to beat the creatures off but they began chasing her also. When they finally returned home, Blanche was gone. She had danced all the way to the city, where she settled down at last. She remained kind and generous all the days of her life, and she walked with a dance in her step.

THIS tale of kindness rewarded made its way with the settlers from

None of your straddling, mincing, saying, but a regular sifter,
cut-the-buckle, chicken flutter set-to. It is good wholesome exercise; and when one of our boys puts his arm around his partner, it's a good hug, and no harm in it.

—*Davy Crockett*

Europe to North America. Earlier forms of the story lacked the dancing details that evolved in the North American version. For these New-World storytellers, dancing was a **metaphor** for life's joy.

In North America, dance was also an opportunity for fellowship and fun. Square dancing was one of the most vital forms of folk dance; it is thought to have developed out of *quadrilles*— four-couple groupings for dancing. Four-couple squares, circles, and two-line longways or contra dance, a dance that is performed in two parallel lines of dancers, are three widespread arrangements for folk dancing. Other forms include couple dancing and line dancing. All of these folk dances developed parallel to one another, and they all coexisted in the early years of North America.

Folk dances create a common link between countries, something that ties them together. But in each country and maybe even each region, the people enlarge on their own individualistic styles, which are then passed from generation to generation.

In America, the early Pilgrims are seldom connected with dancing. We often think of them as sober, staid folk who had

In 1650, a London bookseller named John Playford printed a book titled The *English Dancing Master, or Plaine and Easie Rules for the Dancing of Country Dances, With the Tune to Each Dance*. This was the first time dance steps were written down and published. The book became an overnight bestseller. Included were instruction on circle dances, couple dances, longways dances for four couples, and a few different square dances.

banished any kind of dancing from their society. They trusted in hard work and daily worship. Yet in the writings of English Puritans such as Edmund Spenser, John Milton, and John Bunyan, dancing is spoken of positively. In 1657, Oliver Cromwell, who was a good Puritan, entertained his daughter's wedding guests with dancing.

In the early Puritan settlements in the New World, there was a mixture of opinions on dancing. The misgivings of religious authorities combined with the desires of ordinary people to participate in the fun and exercise of traditional dances. Some strict folk were against dancing, others enjoyed all types of dance, and still others thought it was permissible as long as it did not interfere with work or religious duties.

A bit later in the New England colonies' history, English dancing masters, men who lived and worked like *itinerant* craftsmen, traveled throughout New England, from town to town, looking for those who wanted to learn to dance. Many townsfolk looked to their preacher for permission concerning these dance classes. When allowed to stay, the instructor would rent space, most likely in someone's home and set up a class schedule. This direct encouragement of dancing led to an increase in dancing as a social affair. French dancing masters also came to America. They brought their own practiced steps, including quadrilles, to the dance scene of colonial North America.

After the war of 1812 against the British, many Americans would not dance the English folk dances. However, most ordinary folks in the country continued dancing the steps to which they were accustomed.

> The big circle formation was used for children's party games. While singing old songs or rhymes, children would dance in a large circle. These were common in Southern and Midwestern communities that forbade dancing; they were often called "play parties" rather than dances. The children's movements were accompanied by singing rather than instrumental music.

An American Indian dancer celebrates his cultural and religious heritage.

FOLK DANCE VOCABULARY

Set: The way couples line up for a given dance, such as a big circle, square formation, or longways.

Longways or Contra Set: Two lines of partners facing each other in which the couples move up and down the line performing a sequence of steps with one or two couples who are progressing the opposite way.

Square Set: A formation of four couples facing each other and forming a square. The ensuing dance is then performed in this formation.

Folk dancing in the Appalachian area was not influenced by the itinerant dance masters as much as it was further north in New England. In Appalachia, people enjoyed the folklore they had learned for generations; dancing was no exception. The long-lined contra dances survived here, but mostly in the form of the Virginia Reel, which gradually became a dance for children. Four-couple squares and big circles came in newer dance fashions. A dance sometimes called the Kentucky Running Set, popular in some areas, falls somewhere between the folk dances of England and the square dancing of today.

A folk dance more recently popular in the Appalachian regions is called clogging. It may have begun as the "hornpipe" in the late 18th century, a clog-and-shuffle solo dance imported to North America from England and Scotland. Popular among sailors, the hornpipe often includes *pantomime* related to a

The ¾-time ballroom dance called the waltz swept through both Europe and North America during the 19th century, made popular by the music of composer Johann Strauss. In North America, particularly in the Southwest, folk waltzes spread from Mexico during the reign of the Austrian Maximilian (1864–67). One of these was called the broom waltz, in which the odd man out dances a broom down the center of the room, then snatches the girl of his choice and is pursued by the other male dancers.

sailor's life, such as hauling the anchor or hoisting the sail. The modern form of clogging also combined elements of the square dance and the "buck-and-wing," a solo dance. Clog teams first arose in the mountains of western North Carolina in the 1920s and '30s. Although not danced while actually wearing clogs, clogging is a **percussion** dance, one that is marked by striking the floor so that sound is produced while dancing. Using lively steps and music, clogging music is usually traditional mountain tunes performed with banjos, guitars, and fiddles.

In the 1800s, many North Americans moved west, looking for land, looking for gold,

Native American dances are very structured; each movement carries powerful meaning.

looking for new opportunities. They brought their dancing traditions with them. A new set of dances came to be called the cotillion, which had varying tempos and changing tunes as it moved from part to part. The cotillion began in the ballroom, and it was usually "called" by the fiddler. The caller spontaneously shouted a series of steps that kept the dancers moving in a lively fashion. Adding humorous lines between his calls made any prompter more popular and any dance more enjoyable. More and more, the dancers enjoyed the flexibility of this popular folk dance.

Square dancing's reputation increased until it was being enjoyed at cornhuskings, barn raisings, weddings, and many other

THE HISTORY OF FOLK DANCE

By 1900, folk dancing was not as popular as it had once been—but three years later, Dr. Luther Gulic, athletic director of the New York City schools, added folk dancing to the physical education curriculum. This led to other schools doing the same, so that children were introduced to folk dancing in school gym classes.

Vytautas Beliajus was an American folk dancer, teacher, and editor of a folk-dance magazine. In 1936, he organized a large folk-dance festival in Chicago, and through the 1930s and '40s he organized many more such festivals, where he showcased folk dances from a wide range of world regions. His efforts increased North Americans' appreciation for and understanding of this form of folklore.

The *schottische* is a Scottish dance that was imported from Scotland to Germany, and from there to North America. Eventually, Mexican Americans adopted it as their own. The step is a variation on a basic three rapid steps with a hop. Dancing couples circle the room, then **promenade** and turn around each other.

occasions. Occasionally a spontaneous dance was announced in town on a busy day. In New England, these impromptu get-togethers were called junkets. So that everyone who could come knew of the dance, someone would shout from a central place in town "Junket, junket!" Once a group of people had gathered, the announcer would give the dance's location. Most of these dances were held in individual homes; all the furniture from room to room was pushed up against the wall and the caller stood in a central location.

Meanwhile, Native Americans had very different dance traditions. For them, all things in nature were related to each other. An individual felt within him the same force he saw in the changing of the seasons and the movement of water over rocks in a streambed. This force that touched the wind, the soil, the birds, and human beings was considered sacred; it shaped the native concept of God.

Because of this interconnection between the spirit world and all living things, Native Americans perform ceremonies of thanksgiving for things like rain, harvest, and a successful hunt. They feel a part of the trees, the clouds, and the earth, and they express this sense through their rituals. Dance is an important aspect of most of these sacred ceremonies.

For the American Indian, every dance has deep meaning. From tribe to tribe, costumes, masks, and symbols change, but the dance itself is very similar, a way of performing a story or religious experience. Native dances include much structured movement that has distinct meanings. These steps were handed down from generation to generation. Those who participate and

Immigrants from India have brought new dance traditions to North America.

those who watch understand the dance's meaning as clearly as if they had listened to a story.

The corn dance celebrated the life of the growing corn, so that it might in turn give the people life as a necessary food. Other dances were a part of ceremonies that related to maintaining peace. Storms were sometimes considered to be wars within nature, and if a storm arose while the tribe was performing a peace dance, the people feared misfortune. Songs and dances were acted out in appeals for clear skies, which were a symbol of peace.

Native festivals of joy also included dance. Times when the hunt had been successful or the harvest plentiful, the dancers enjoyed fellowship and hope that they were secure together for another season. Some of these dances were elaborate and included props of trees or branches, feathers or masks, and much celebration.

Although Native Americans and European Americans danced for different reasons, across North America, people still dance to celebrate special days of the year, new seasons, or other special events. Although the dances we have reviewed are particularly associated with North America, we will study in the following chapters the diverse cultural dances that are also a part our heritage because of the many different cultures that now reside in North America's "melting pot."

The maypole is an ancient dance custom from Northern Europe.

TWO

Northern European
Folk Dances
Fertility and Fun

Welsh dancers honor their Celtic culture.

ONCE UPON A TIME there lived a beautiful girl—but she was very lazy and hated to do any kind of work. She was so unhappy when she had to spin that if she found one tiny knot in her flax, she would pull out everything she had spun and throw it onto the floor.

The girl had a servant who was very industrious. She worked hard and long to get her work done. Anything that her mistress damaged, the young servant made right. So on the day that the beautiful girl threw the flax all over the floor, the servant gathered it up, washed it, spun it, and then had a beautiful dress woven out of it. The dress was to be hers and she was very happy about it.

The lazy girl was soon to marry a young man who had been courting her for some time. The night before the wedding, the servant girl danced merrily around in the dress she had made. The dress was very beautiful and the servant girl was happy to be able to wear it.

The bride-to-be watched her for a while and then said, "How well you can jump about over that dress that you scraped up from my waste."

The bridegroom heard her talking to the servant and he asked what she meant. So the lazy bride told him that the dress was made from some flax that she had thrown away. As the bridegroom watched the servant dance, he realized that the servant girl was both diligent and light-hearted—while his intended wife was just plain lazy. "Will you dance with me?" he asked the servant girl. And as they skipped and twirled, he decided not to marry the lazy girl and instead chose the servant as his wife. The young girl's dance of happiness changed her life forever.

Dance can be very important in the lives of those who participate in it. Dancing is a language of its own. Without saying a word, dancers can create a mood, share a message, and evoke emotion among themselves or within the people watching them. Dancing can also be a simple act of pleasure felt at a special moment.

THE Morris dance was a folk dance performed by men in rural England. These men were chosen and trained not only to dance but also to perform various other customs, including **mumming**. The costumes worn by the Morris dancers helped to unify them in spirit. The steps are an up and down jig with occasional

When foreign ambassadors came to England they were surprised by the popularity of dancing among every class within the country. They often referred to the English as the "dancing English."

Morris dancers in England.

Scottish dance festivals allow dancers times of celebration, physical exercise, and cultural connection.

high leaps. The dance may have originally celebrated the revival of a pagan god after his death. It is linked to fertility, magic, and luck.

The original Morris dancers may have blackened their faces as a ritual disguise. Disguising themselves so that those watching the dance would not recognize them is a common practice among folk dancers throughout the world. By becoming anonymous, dancers can better express to watchers the dances' spiritual significance.

One figure that is a part of the Morris dance is an animal-man. His role varies in different dances. In the horn dance, a  dance procession with six dancers moves in a formal manner carrying deer antlers, along with a Maid Marian and a fool, a hobby-horse, and a youth with a crossbow. The youth then "shoots" at the leading stag dancers (those carrying the horns) as they proceed.

Ancient rites performed for crop fertility

included dances called the hilt and point. These dances told a story in almost play-like form. Swords that were interlocked at their points were used to look like they had beheaded one of the performers. Then the physician revived that person. The dance was thought to bring good luck and it was performed across Europe. Like the hilt dance, a mock sacrifice was made to ensure fertility, success in battle, and defense against evil spirits. The swords of between five and eight dancers were stepped and jumped over until they formed a star-shaped design, and a pretend beheading occurred. Sword dances are still very popular among Scottish immigrants to North America. These dancers are also well known for the "Highland leap." These high leaps emphasize elevation while keeping a stiff upper body, very unlike other dances that tend to include graceful flowing leaps.

Swedish immigrants to North America brought other dances with them. The oldest of the Swedish dances is the circle or chain formation. Dances like these were danced either clockwise or counterclockwise around bonfires, maypoles, and at weddings. Dancers can all see one another and are able to share equally in the fun. Couples performed the *polska,* another popular Swedish dance. The partners held on to one another and turned around and around, employing a harmonizing step in three-quarter time. Some polskas include men turning cart-

During the time of the Christmas and New Year holidays, mummers dressed in costumes, including masks, and performed small plays for entertainment. The players used dance as they moved from house to house, wishing villagers well and enjoying social visits with one another.

Folk dances have led to the creation of many modern forms of dance. For instance, tap dance come from the hornpipe, brought from the British Isles, combined with African American folk dance traditions.

Scottish dancers compete, demonstrating their skills.

wheels and somersaults while others bend their knees while dancing.

Among Irish North Americans, the jig is a popular folk dance. Jigs can be danced as a solo or couples dance, but the solo dance form is most popular in North America. The jig allows the dancer to demonstrate intricate footwork; the dancer hops on one foot while drawing patterns in the air with the other foot.

Mixing a long history with tradition, dance offered the common people of Northern Europe an escape from everyday life. Festivals brought people together; these celebrations included a chance to dress up and eat well—and an opportunity to dance.

MORRIS DANCE SETS

The Bean Dance
The Leap Frog
Laudnum Bunches
Shepherd's Hey (this is a solo Morris jig)

Dances from Eastern Europe have influenced modern dance performances.

THREE

Eastern European
Folk Dances
Power and Beauty

The ancient roots of traditional European dance steps can be glimpsed in today's ice skating performances.

Long Ago There was a czar who had three sons. When they were about to be married, the czar decided to give them a challenge.

"Shoot an arrow as far as you can and wherever it lands is where you will find your bride."

The eldest brother shot his arrow toward the village. It landed in the lawyer's yard. He would marry the lawyer's daughter.

The second brother shot his arrow on the gardener's roof. He would marry the gardener's daughter.

The youngest son, Ivan the Fool, shot his arrow toward the sun. After days of looking for it, Ivan found the arrow in a swamp with a large green frog sitting on it.

"Marry me," the frog said.

"I can't marry a frog," Ivan said.

"You must," said the frog.

So he married the frog, and his brothers married their wives the next week.

Not long after, the czar told his sons he had a test for who would inherit his kingdom. "Have your wives sew me a shirt by the morning. Whoever has married the best seamstress will become the czar."

Ivan was very upset when he told his wife about the test.

"Have no worries, Ivan," the frog wife said. "Morning is wiser than evening."

That night the frog wife went into the garden, peeled off her frog skin, and became a beautiful princess. Clapping her hands, twirling and dancing, she asked that a shirt be sewn better than any the czar had ever seen.

In the morning, the czar was most pleased with the frog wife's shirt. He was worried, however, at having a frog as the czarina, so he devised another test.

"Whoever's wife bakes the best loaf of bread will become the next czar," he said.

Again Ivan worried as he told his frog wife.

"Have no worries, Ivan," the frog wife said, "Morning is wiser than evening."

The two other wives were suspicious of the frog so they decided to watch her that night and follow everything she did. When the frog wife saw them hiding in the kitchen she knocked a potted plant into some dough and kneaded it by jumping up and down.

When they finally left, she peeled off her frog skin. Clapping her hands, twirling, and dancing, she asked that bread be baked better than any the czar had ever tasted.

Again the czar loved the frog wife's offering best—but again he questioned the wisdom of having a frog as the czarina.

"There will be one more test. Tonight we will have a feast to see which wife dances the best. She will be the new czarina."

Once more Ivan worried to tell his wife of the czar's test.

"Have no worries, Ivan. Go without me and when you hear a loud noise do not be scared. Tell everyone that your wife is coming."

At the dance that night, Ivan's brothers teased him about his wife. Then suddenly there was a loud noise and the whole palace shook.

"That's my wife," Ivan said, calming the guests.

Polish princess Marie Nicolaewnais is believed to have created the polka-mazur, which was closely linked to a waltz. The dance was done with brass metal heels that were struck while dancing. Some believe the mazurka is the most beautiful dance of all time because of its sweetness, tenderness, and grace. The movements are always made sideways in an easy manner.

Soon a golden coach arrived at the palace. Out stepped the frog wife as a beautiful princess.

"Your love has broken the spell that was cast on me at birth," the frog wife said to Ivan.

Now the other wives were very upset and planned to follow the dance steps of the frog wife, hoping to still become the czarina.

While eating, the frog wife poured wine down one sleeve and put chicken bones down the other sleeve. The other wives did the same.

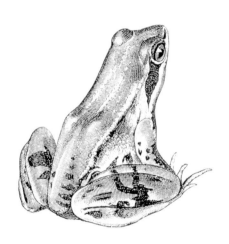

The frog wife and Ivan captivated the guests during the dance. When they finished, she waved her arms and two doves flew to the czar's right and left shoulders. Then the two wives danced but as they waved their arms wine splattered in the czar's face and chicken bones hit him in the head.

"Enough," the czar yelled. "No more tests. To my youngest son and his beautiful wife, I leave my land. May you live long and prosper."

IN this Russian folk tale, the frog princess enchants her audience not only because of her dancing ability but also because she possesses true loveliness beneath her ugly frog skin. Her dance reveals the truth; it is what gives her both power and beauty.

Like other countries, Russia enjoys a rich heritage of folk dancing. Male Russian dancers, however, did not whirl or leap. Instead, their steps included much bowing. They also bent their knees and rose suddenly, **pirouetting** and moving the arms and hips. Meanwhile, the women's dance was more of a walk than a dance. One dance called the *makovitza* or Dance of Cakes was performed as a harvest dance, demonstrating thanksgiving for the year's crops. During this dance, girls each carried a cake made of honey and poppy seeds. As the dance progressed, the cake was eaten to the rhythm of their steps, whether fast or slow.

The *polonaise* became very popular in Russia when soldiers brought it from Poland. This dance was not an opportunity for interaction between the sexes, since originally only fighting men participated in this triumphal march of the old warriors. As the dance evolved, however, women also danced it but only with each other.

Although popular in Russia, the polonaise was not the primary folk dance in Poland. Instead, the polka was an intrinsic part of the Polish heritage, one that crossed the ocean to the New World.

Some believe this peasant dance originated in Czechoslovakia during the early 1800s. According to tradition, a young servant woman named Anna Chadimova did the lively dance in two-quarter time and named it the polka because it reminded her of Polish women she had seen dance with a skip and a slide. The polka was invented to dance to the common people's music.

When the polka was introduced in France and England, it be-

Folk dances provided material that could be used in ballet. When parts of the mazurka or the tarantella or any other folk dances are added to an act in a ballet, it is called character dancing. The mazurka has also been adopted by Tex-Mex dancers in the Southwest.

came a huge success. From there it moved to the United States. Some variations of the polka include the Heel and Toe Polka, Polka-Waltz, Polka-Coquette, and Polka-Redowa. As they danced the polka, couples did a series of fast chases around the room, occasional turning as they went. The *galop* was a dance similar to the polka, but this dance's horse-like galloping was a faster paced form of the polka.

For the Polish people, dancing was a part of many of the celebration days. Before the beginning of **Lent**, numerous parties called *karnawat*—carnival time—were enjoyed. Dancing, music, and food were everywhere; sometimes these festivals lasted for days.

Even remembering the dead was cause for dancing and celebration. For instance, in memory of Saint Martin, who was elected Pope in 649, the Polish people had a feast day. They ate goose to commemorate Saint Martin's killing of flocks of geese to feed the people during a time of famine. After eating, the celebration continued with music and dancing.

No wedding ceremony among the Polish people was complete without dancing. The bride and groom performed some of these traditional dances with an **intermediary**. Then the bridesmaids and groomsmen joined. The guests took part in other wedding dancing as they enjoyed a party filled with polkas, music, food, and drink. At the end of the party, the marriage cap was placed on the bride's head. She then danced with all the married women, symbolizing her acceptance into their position. The bride was then

In the early 1700s in Russia, the Grand Duchess Yelizaveta Petrovna helped reestablish folk dance as part of the nobility's social activity. Because she had been cared for as a child by ordinary Russian women and girls, the Grand Duchess learned folk dances like the *khorovod* or ring dance. She also listened to the folk tales shared by her caretakers. According to legend, she danced a folk dance at a formal ball; considered shocking at the time, her behavior helped revive the folk dance culture.

given to the groom; after he danced with her again, he allowed her to dance with all the men before the last dance between him and his new wife at the end of the wedding. This moment of dance and celebration was the beginning of a new life for both bride and groom.

In Romania, dancers enjoyed the chain dance, where dancers stood in a line all facing the same direction with linked arms. Many of these dances begin at a slow pace and gradually increase in speed. Finally, partners turn around and around.

The *kolo* is a chain dance from Serbia and Croatia. North Americans of Serbian and Croatian descent perform as many as 15 different kolo dances. The dancers hold hands, elbows, fingers, or waists, and the steps include hops, springs, jumps, stamps, and claps. One kolo is performed during the kneading of the wedding cake. Dancers rotate around the baker or around the oven as the cake bakes. During another kolo, a dance of fertility, the leader is a young girl carrying a snake.

Across Eastern Europe dance influenced celebrations in many ways. For immigrants from these lands to North America, these traditional dances still bring joy and meaning to life's important moments.

Traditional Southern European folk dances create modern entertainment for both spectators and participants.

FOUR

Southern European
Folk Dances
Reason to Celebrate

A Spanish dancer demonstrates flamenco steps.

ONCE THERE WAS A very rich king who had three handsome sons. Although he loved his sons very much, the king insisted that everyone, including his sons, obey his orders.

One day the three sons went visiting without asking permission. As a punishment, the king turned them into rabbits, the eldest a pinto, the second a white, and the youngest a little green rabbit. As he did so he told them, "You will not leave the palace for one year and you will only be a human at night during that time."

While nibbling grass in the palace garden, the green rabbit said, "Brothers, let's crawl through the water pipe and escape."

The other rabbits were afraid to try, but the green rabbit insisted. When they were free, they hopped over hills and back again. As they returned later that evening, they heard a beautiful voice singing.

"Let's go find who is singing so beautifully," said the green rabbit.

But this time the other rabbits refused to go. So the green rabbit went alone. He found a huge palace, and inside the garden he saw a beautiful princess singing. With one swoop, the princess captured the green rabbit. She showed him to her parents and then took him to her room.

Suddenly, the rabbit spoke. "Beautiful princess, I am not really a rabbit but a prince who has been enchanted. If I do not go home to my father tonight he will kill me. If you release me I will return as soon as my punishment is over."

The kind princess let the rabbit go, even though she had already fallen in love with him.

LOCAL GREEK VILLAGE DANCES

Cretan dances are quick, forceful, and proud.
Arcadian dances use wide steps, high leaps, and heavy
   ground stomping
Thessalian dances are calm, cool, and proud
Epirus dances are monotonous and austere, expressing
   the agony of their slavery during the Ottoman Empire

Much time passed and the rabbit did not return. The princess
was very heartbroken; in order to cheer her up her parents decided to give a great *fiesta* of music and dancing in her honor.

In a nearby village lived a man with a daughter named Rosita.
She could sing joyous songs while playing her guitar. Rosita and
her father decided to visit the princess to sing for her. But on the
way they stopped in the city where the rabbits lived. Rosita
peeked into the window of the palace and saw a bedroom with
three beautiful beds. As Rosita watched, she saw three rabbits
jump into the beds. As each one rolled over, he turned into a
handsome prince. The first two fell instantly asleep but the third
began to cry.

His brothers woke and said, "Forget the princess. Father will
never let you marry her."

The three princes finally slept and Rosita crept away. When
she arrived at the princess's palace, Rosita sang and danced but
the princess remained solemn. Then as Rosita danced, she acted
out the story of the green rabbit and his brothers.

When Rosita finished the dance of the green rabbit and his

Southern European folk dance is kept alive today in performances on stage and at community festivals.

brothers, the princess was overjoyed. She begged her parents to let her go see him. As she hid with Rosita, she watched each rabbit become a prince. As soon as the green rabbit changed, the princess could not wait any longer so she ran to him.

Just then the king passed by and saw her. He was very angry. When they told him they wanted to marry, he agreed only if the prince remained a rabbit for seven more years and the princess filled seven barrels with tears and wore out seven pairs of iron shoes. They agreed.

The princess left in tears. After walking long enough to wear out the shoes and fill the barrels with tears, she arrived at the house of the moon. She was so tired she asked his help to reach the green rabbit's house.

"*Niña*, I cannot go there now but my friend the sun will help you."

When she told the sun the story, he said that people were praying for him to shine because in three days the green rabbit would marry someone the king had chosen.

"Señor Sol, please take me to the palace."

"I cannot take you because if I held you, you would burn, but my friend the wind will help you."

Again the princess told the wind the story. Señor Air told her he had just destroyed the green rabbit's wedding because the rabbit had been in the chapel praying for the return of his true love. "Grab hold of my waist," the wind told the princess, "and I will answer both your prayers."

FOUR CATEGORIES OF THE FLAMENCO

Jondo is a deep, serious, and melancholy expression that is the most difficult to understand and perform.

Intermedio is not as difficult to perform properly. It is also not as moving as the jondo.

Chico is frivolous, tender, vivacious, sometimes sad, and often joyful. It is not usually done with precision in mind but rather with joyful fun.

Popular is a commercialized version of all forms of the flamenco. There is nothing off-limits and the meaning is not conveyed to the viewer.

Within minutes, she was at the green rabbit's palace. She showed the king the tears and the shoes, and they were married at a big fiesta with dancing and music. They lived a long life together, full of joy and singing and dancing.

As this fanciful Spanish folktale indicates, the Spanish connect dancing with celebration and joy. Theirs is a long and great heritage of dancing, for whenever there is reason to celebrate there is reason to dance. Many Spaniards believe that dancing is in their blood.

Like many other folk dances whose roots are spread across the world, the Spanish flamenco can be traced to other countries, including, Morocco, Egypt, Israel, and Pakistan. The Gypsies have been credited with keeping the song and dance alive in Spain.

THE TRAGIC DANCE OF ZALONGA

In 1821, Greek Zalonga women who were trapped on a mountain by the Turks performed a dance in which they leaped thousands of feet to their deaths. The women, knowing they would be sold into slavery, joined hands with each other and their children and danced toward the edge of the mountain, finally choosing death over the humiliation of capture.

Gypsies are an ancient ethnic group that originated long ago in northern India. **Nomads** who were persecuted for years in Spain, they traveled across Europe and even to North America. Their heritage of religious folk music influenced the dance that became the flamenco.

The *cante jondo*, the main form of the dance, expresses the suffering of the people. Their sufferings included imprisonment, chain gangs, death, and torture. With a spirit unbroken by persecution, the Gypsies developed a folk dance that was filled with expression and story. Male and female participants each danced in their own way. The *bailaor* or male dancer emphasized footwork, while the *bailaora*, the female dancer, danced with her upper torso, the "dance of the arms."

During the 19th century, the Catalan people of northeast Spain fought to gain their independence. During this time, an old folk dance called the *sardana* began to be popular among those fighting and eventually became a symbol of the Catalan rebellion. The dance brought the people together and offered them a unity that they could express outwardly among themselves.

Dance was important in other parts of Southern Europe as well. For the ancient Greeks, for example, dance indicated their cultural status. They believed not only in the education of dance but they used dance along with drama to support political views. Even the philosopher Plato wrote in favor of dance when he said, "to sing well and to dance well is to be well educated. Noble dances should confer on the student not only health and agility and beauty, but also goodness of the soul and a well-balanced mind."

Of course, Plato was speaking of formal dance, that dance that was taught as a part of a higher education or socially performed in the theatre. But for the ancient Greeks, dance was not only formal; it was also an informal celebration of life's joy. They believed that dance was a gift from the gods, and dance was a way to communicate with the gods.

Like all people who perform folk dances, the Greek dancers express emotions and share the feelings of pride they feel as a

In ancient times, dance, song, and music were all integral parts of the Greek theater. In fact, the Greeks used the same word for both dance and song. The English words chorus, chorale, choir, and choreography all come from this same word. Ancient Greek literature contains numerous references to dancing.

nation. Joy, sadness, hope, and fun are just a few of these feelings. Their dances can be grouped into war dances, religious dances, and peace dances. War dances are believed to be the oldest of all dances. Through these dances, warriors were inspired and prepared for victory. Men with weapons danced in order to get their bodies, minds, and spirits ready to defend their people. Both men and women performed religious dances. These serious, calm, and simple dances were performed around the altar of the honored god as a thanksgiving for providing needs. Finally, peace dances were either theatrical or social dances that were enjoyed at weddings, funerals, and other social events.

Today, Greek immigrants to North America still perform their ancient dances in circles. The dancers form a human chain by holding on to one another by the hands, waists, or shoulders. Then they move in unison. The dance leader moves the chain from place to place as the dance progresses. Traditionally, the chain dancers take position according to seniority. Men usually come first, then women. Age and status are then ranked within these groups.

In the Greek villages of Thrace and Macedonia an annual event called Anastenaria is held where 12 men who have fully prepared themselves carry *icons* of Saint Helen and Saint Constantine and dance barefoot on lighted coals. As they dance, they pray that Saint Constantine will give them strength to confront and get rid of evil spirits that exist at the gates of their village. Scientists from all parts of the world who have observed the ritual cannot explain the absence of burns on the dancers' bare feet. This deeply religious dance is apparently an example of the power of the mind over the body.

SOMETIMES dance speaks an individual's deepest feeling. At other times dance can be the expression of an entire people. The flashy dances of the Gypsies from Spain and the amazing feats of the hot coal dancers of Greece show a great diversity in spirit. These dances are not one person's work but they are a combination of many people's creativity over many years, the fruit of their customs, their beliefs, and even their way of thinking. This Southern European heritage has enriched North America as well.

A traditional Mexican folk dance.

FIVE

Mexican and
South American
Folk Dances
Flavor and Richness

Dancers in the Mexican Ballet Folklórico wear elaborate costumes that reflect the culture of each region in Mexico.

ONCE THERE WAS an owl that was very shy. Owl also believed he was very ugly. So he never came out during the daylight. He only came out at night.

One night he met a young woman. They started talking and she invited him to her house. There they sat for hours talking. Because they enjoyed each other so much, the young woman invited him back the next night. Night after night Owl returned to her porch, where they talked and talked.

The young woman's friends asked why Owl only came to visit her at night.

"He works very hard and by the time he gets home, eats, and changes it is after dark.

"Well, he can't work on Sunday," they said. "Why don't you have a party so we can all meet him?"

The young woman thought this was a great idea. So she told Owl she was having a party in his honor.

Owl was surprised and happy by the thought of a party just for him. But when the day of the party arrived he was very nervous. He invited his cousin Rooster to come with him. When he looked at rooster, Owl became more scared. Rooster was tall and had bright clothing, but Owl was drab. He was ugly.

"Rooster, you go ahead to the party. I have forgotten something and will be right back." Owl stayed away until dark, and even then he came with a large sombrero that covered his head.

Once inside, Owl heard the music of the drummers and the singers, and he realized they were playing his favorite song. Owl wanted to dance. He no longer felt shy, so he found the young woman and they began dancing. Owl loved dancing and he was very good. They danced all night long.

Owl forgot about the time until he heard his cousin Rooster trying to crow. Rooster was drunk and he had missed the sunrise. Owl ran from the room, banging into the door on his way out. He fell to the floor and his hat slipped off.

Jumping onto the back of his horse, Owl left. The young woman called after him. "Owl, come back!" But Owl never heard her.

The young woman went back to the house and cleaned up. She thought of how Owl looked. She liked his big eyes and his round face. She didn't know he thought he was ugly. For a whole year she waited every night, hoping he would come back. But he never did. Finally she met someone else and married him. But even then she would think about Owl and wonder why he had run away and where he had gone.

THIS Mexican folktale shows the power of dance. Dancers reveal the true beauty of their natures, a beauty that is more than skin deep. Dance frees us from our inhibitions. Dance has a way of equalizing all other concerns. It tells a story all its own.

> In Brazil, the *samba* is a fast-moving dance that is practiced for months before an annual event.

In Mexico, the cowboys danced the heel-stamping *zapateado*. Someone would play the guitar, while others sang and danced outside or on the floor of the bunkhouse. For men who spent long hot hours on horseback, a chance to enjoy another kind of physical exercise brought pleasure. It made lonely nights far from their homes and families more bearable.

The Ballet Folklórica.

The *ballet folklórico* are folk dance groups that perform traditional Mexican regional dances. Dancers in these performances wear elaborate costumes typical of the traditional dress of Mexico's various states. The dances are accompanied by **mariachi** music. In the 1950s, *El Ballet Folkórico de Mexico*, the official cultural representative of the Mexican government, was founded, and it tours North America as a symbol of Mexico's cultural identity. Folklórico groups are common in many Mexican American communities; they are often made up of college students and young children, and they perform at community events, school celebrations, and political holidays.

El *carnavalito* is a dance of all the people. The Argentine poorer rural people dance it as well as those who frequent the dance halls and ballrooms of the towns. During festivals in the hills of Jujuy and Salta, men and women dance around musicians. This is a chain or circle dance; the group leader may carry a handkerchief.

Dance—*el baile*—is one of the most important social traditions in Mexico and the Southwest. In the days when communities were isolated, dances were important social and cultural events. Courtship took place at these dances, and families and relatives had the chance to interact and exchange news. Many Mexican ballads, legends, and jokes are set in dances, where some of life's most exciting events took place. Holiday celebrations still include a community dance.

Hispanic immigrants to North America have brought with

Folklórica dancers.

The Ballet Folklórico demonstrates traditional Mexican costumes and folk dances.

Handclapping is an important part of the *cueca,* which is a Chilean dance for couples. Singer and dancers emphasize the music with clapping.

them a rich heritage of dance. These dances have influenced popular modern dances. For instance, the tango is a dance that originated in South America. Popular in Argentina, it probably began as an old folk dance called the *milonga,* with influences from African and Cuban dance as well. Because of its popularity even today, its roots as a folk dance are often forgotten.

Many South American dances have a religious element. The Cobeua Indians from Brazil dance a fertility dance that includes foot stamping and singing. Religious dances in the Caribbean include the popular vodou dancing. These dances combine African beliefs with Catholicism. Dancers shake their heads and shoulders so violently that they sometimes collapse. Drums, rattles, bamboo tubes, and an iron plate called an *ogan* accompany the dancers. Many of these dances are performed in secret.

Folk dance is often informal; these dancers are celebrating on the beach in Colombia.

The limbo is another South American dance that has become popular across North America, often danced at parties. When Hispanic Americans dance the limbo, they do many fancy steps, competing and showing off for one another. Dancing under a stick that is held closer and closer to the ground takes great agility that has to be built up over a long time. To do this dance well takes long hours of practice.

Skill and time are a part of many Mexican and South American folk dances. Costumes and tradition add color and meaning to the steps and sets of each dance. As these dances travel north to the United States and Canada, they add flavor and richness to parties and celebrations.

The Jewish faith uses music and movement to celebrate their faith.

SIX

Jewish Folk Dances

Praising God

Expressing worship through movement is one of the most common religious experiences.

FOR JEWS, worshipping God through dance is based on various texts of the Bible. Used as a way of worship and praise, celebrating God's blessing through movement is both reverent and joyful. As with many forms of dance, Jewish festivals and celebrations are occasions for community excitement. Ordinary people use their bodies' movements to strengthen their relationship with God.

The Bible tells that when the Israelites had crossed the Red Sea to escape the Pharaoh's armies, "Miriam the prophetess, Aaron's sister, took a tambourine in her hand, and all the women followed her, with tambourines and dancing" (Exodus 15:20). And then again after David's famous battle with the giant Goliath "the women came out from all the towns of Israel to meet King Saul with singing and dancing, with joyful songs and with tambourines and lutes" (1 Samuel 18:6).

One form of ancient Hebrew folk dancing was similar to folk dancing or square dancing. Called the *sher*, this dance usually took place outside. The women formed a separate group from the men; the sexes only danced among themselves, not with each other. Some people believe this was a tailor's dance originally and the steps represented a pair of shears and the threading of a needle.

There are many Jewish dances that surround the wedding ceremony. One has to do with the custom of cutting the bride's hair the night before the wedding; another, the Broiges dance, is a mock argument between the bride's mother and mother-in-law. At the end of the dance, they make up; the mothers hope to

A folk dance is a dance that has been created by the people, for the people and a large part of the public should be dancing it.

—Gurit Kadman, the mother of the modern Israeli Folk Dances Movement

teach the newlyweds an important lesson as they begin their new life.

Today, in North American orthodox Jewish weddings, men and women still dance separately, enjoying traditional songs and dances, such as the *hora*. During the dancing, wedding guests often raise the bride and groom on chairs. According to Jewish traditions, it is a mitzvah—a good deed commanded by God—to make the bride and groom happy on their wedding day. Dancing adds to the joyfulness of the occasion.

Jewish folk dances express in their movement and rhythm the Jewish people's connection to the past and to the present. Traditionally, they mirrored the Jews' important values: for instance, the Bible, working the land, holidays and tradition, and the unity of the Jewish people. Often, music and rhythm are more important than any particular dance steps.

Dance was a way for Jews to hold on to their identity, despite being scattered across the world. When the state of Israel formed

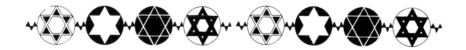

L'chaim—to life! This affirmation is a basic tenet of the Jewish faith, and is expressed as well in traditional Jewish dances.

JEWISH DANCE TERMS

Bulgar: One of the most common American-Jewish dance and tune genres, it is a circle, line, or couple dance. Its best-known step is similar to the Israeli dance called the hora.

Freylekhs: A lively circle or line dance in 4/4 rhythm, the most common in East European Jewish wedding dances.

Sher: One of the most common Jewish dance forms, similar to a square dance or a quadrille.

in the 1940s, Jews sought to assert their unique identity in many ways, including through dance. Since many of their ancient religious dances had been lost over the years, they created a new form of Jewish dance that was created out of dance elements originating in the various native countries of the Jewish immigrants (for example, Romania or Russia). They leaned heavily on the Old Testament scriptures as a source for shaping these "new" folk dances. These dances were social and *secular*, and yet they wove *theology* and fun together. According to one Jewish writer, Gurith Kadman, the source of Israeli dancing was the "earth, labour and the resurgence of the Jewish nation."

These dances give Jews a sense of both their history and their religious heritage. For exam-

Let them praise his name with dancing. . . .

—*Psalm 149:3*

ple, on Shavu'oth, the day of thanksgiving, Jews may dance to songs whose lyrics go back to the days of the Jewish pioneers before Israel was founded. On what is known as Jerusalem Day (the day of the reunification of Jerusalem as a result of the Six Day War in 1967) Jews may dance to songs whose lyrics have to do with Jerusalem.

Jewish dance is rooted in the past—the long-ago past of Bible days and the more recent past of the nation of Israel. These folk dances give unity and hope to a people who are still spread across the world. They connect Jews to their heritage of faith and courage.

African dances connect participants with the forces of nature.

SEVEN

African Folk Dance
A Powerful Force

Inside this elaborate Nigerian costume is a dancer, called the "Guardian of the Night."

ONCE THERE WAS a great drought and all of the riverbeds and springs were dry. Lion, Tiger, Wolf, Jackal, Rabbit, and Elephant met to decide on a plan.

"Let's go to the riverbed and dance," someone suggested. "By beating the ground, we can bring the water to the surface."

Everyone loved that idea except Rabbit. "I will not dance to bring water up," he said. "That is a crazy idea."

But all the other animals began dancing. They danced and danced and danced. Finally, the water reached the surface. Everyone drank as much as they could, but since Rabbit did not dance, he was not allowed any water. Rabbit just laughed at them.

The next morning the animals saw Rabbit's foot tracks leading down to the river. They met again to decide what to do.

Tortoise said, "I will catch Rabbit."

"How can you catch him?" the other animals asked.

Tortoise told them to put tar all over his shell. He would then go down to the river and sit on the edge.

"I will look like a rock and when Rabbit steps on me he will be stuck."

The animals agreed with Tortoise's plan. That night Rabbit arrived at the river to get a drink.

"Well," he said, "look at the rock the animals have placed here so I will not have to get my feet wet."

Rabbit put his left foot on the rock. It stuck. Tortoise stuck his head out.

"Ha! Rabbit! I've got you."

African dancers from the Hulis tribe.

"No, you don't," Rabbit said. "I still have three more feet to get away." But each time he tried to get unstuck, one more foot held tight to the surface.

Tortoise slowly crawled with Rabbit on his back to where the other animals waited. They told Rabbit that his insults to them did not pay. Now he would have to die. But how?

"Rabbit, how should we kill you?" they asked.

"Just don't bring me to a shameful death," he said.

"What death is that?" they asked.

"Do not take me by my tail and dash my head against a stone, please don't do this."

"This is how you will die," they decided. Lion would perform the killing, because he was the most powerful one.

Lion stood up, picked up Rabbit, and grabbed him firmly by the tail. As he swung him around, the white skin slipped off of Rabbit and he was free.

If you can talk, you can sing. If you can walk, you can dance.

—*African Proverb*

BODY ATTACHMENTS

Leg rattles like the seapod rattle of Zimbabwe, the thigh bell of Kenya, and the metal anklet bells of Ghana add a different accompaniment for ritualistic dancing. Controlling the rhythm of these attachments requires skill and practice.

As this African folktale indicates, Africans believed that dancing was a powerful force that could shape reality. (Perhaps the only thing as powerful was the trickery of a sly mind like Rabbit's!)

Like Native Americans, Africans felt they were a part of all of nature. They believed in spirits that lived within animals, the earth, vegetation, and humans. Africans acted this relationship

Traditional African American dances are rooted in Africa.

Dancers in a vodou ceremony in Haiti reflect their African roots.

DANCE STEPS

Ikpo Okme dancers hop from one foot to the other.
Ebenebe dancers do a stamping pattern that leads into a
   cartwheel.
Iza dancers stand straight and perform high kicks
Nkpopi dancers do a leaping dance
Etukwa lean their torso parallel to the earth and drum
   their feet in a staccato beat
Nazaukwu Nabi dancers stamp their feet with sudden
   pauses

Talley Beatty, a leading figure in modern African American dance, created a series of folk-inspired dances for performance.

out in their dances. Like the animals of this folktale, they believed they could communicate with nature and with spirits through their dances.

In Africa, the tree-worship dance is an example of the way Africans feel toward nature. Men circle the tree, keeping the rhythm of the music. They raise their head and arms toward the top of the tree branches, leaves, and fruit before running their hands down along the tree trunk. At the bottom of the tree, the dancers humble themselves, hoping that the strength of the tree will become their own.

African tribal dances vary from tribe to tribe and region to region. Where men and women live in arid areas, the hard dry ground echoes with the sounds of their dancing feet, while those living in marshlands dance with a rhythm that flows like that of the wet lands and water surrounding them.

The cakewalk is a strutting, high-stepping dance that was once popular among African American slaves. It was actually a **parody** of white ballroom dancing, but by the end of the 19th century, it had become a ballroom dance in its own right. Couples formed a square, with men on the inside and women on the outside, and judges awarded fancy cakes to the best dancers—creating the expression, "That takes the cake." The cakewalk also influenced the development of ragtime and jazz dance steps.

In February of each year, the Ngoni tribe of Zambia celebrates N'cwala. This is a harvest observance in which the
tribe offers the Ngoni chief the first produce of the year.
Twelve local tribes participate in a kind of dance competition. Each group is comprised of the best dancers. As
the men perform for the highest chief, the king of the
entire Ngoni people, the women of their tribe encircle
them, clapping and singing songs to encourage them.
The king chooses one tribe as having the best warrior
dancers. The dance tells the story of how the warriors
would protect their chief in case of war.

Most of the patterns acted out in dance are a continuous repeating of a simple beat. Instruments keep time and may be
played by those accompanying the dancers or by the dancers
themselves. The Angus of West Africa dance a circle dance called
the *rumada*. As they dance repetitive steps in a circular pattern,
they blow 14 large buffalo horns.

Each dance is performed for a specific purpose. For example,
when the Akan of Ghana dance the *abofor,* they want to appease
the spirit of the dangerous beast they have just killed. The dance
tells a story so that the community learns from the movements of
the participants how the kill occurred. Dancing after a successful
hunt is a common practice among the tribes, and ample food is a
source of deep contentment.

Men are the primary dancers in most of Africa. Many dances
are intended to enhance their masculinity. When women and
men dance at the same time, they usually remain separate.

Dancers from Mozambique.

A vodou dancer from Haiti.

Sometimes there are two different circles or sometimes the dance positions are dissimilar, one standing erect while the other is bent toward the ground. Aside from fertility rituals or mating dances, there is not usually any physical contact between male and female dancers.

Some dancing is performed to move community members into action. Nigerian fishermen from the Nupe tribe dance with net throwing as a part of the ritual. For them, net throwing is a part of their everyday lives as well. The dance reinforces the importance of perfecting this skill.

Women are reminded of their place within the tribe by dances that are performed at night. These reinforce the role of the male and female in a particular tribe. Initiation dances prepare young men and women for adulthood. They also encourage these young people to perfect

Men dance for blessings of fertility, health, and honor. Women sometimes participate in special healing dances intended to cast out evil spirits. Dancing can bring healing to individuals and to the tribe as a whole.

When someone dies in the Owo-Yoruba tribe, the young men perform a dance called the *Igogo*. Once the person has been buried and covered over with the earth, the men stamp and dance to pack down the dirt.

certain tasks that prove they are prepared to move into their new life roles—marriage, provision, and family.

Many religious dances use masks to identify the roles the dancers play. Some dancers represent gods and others portray ancestors. The Tyiwara spirit masqueraders of Bambara use masks made to look like antelopes and other wild animals. While carrying these masks and imitating how the animals move in the wild, the dancers hope to increase the fertility of their crops and people. The more elaborate and heavy the mask, the less the dancers are able to move, indicating that the mask is more critical to the significance of the dance than the steps themselves.

Physical feats may also be a part of African dance. Because dance is a popular form of recreation as well as a religious rite, practicing steps and moves can lead to a competition between tribal members; they aim toward strengthening and improving skills. Some tribes accomplish gymnastic skills while dancing. Leaps, somersaults, and cartwheels are done with amazing height and dexterity. Many dances that go on for hours or even days are proof of extreme endurance.

Children take part in dancing in Africa as a kind of education, much like physical education in North American schools. Dancing teaches skill, but it also helps with coordination. Some dances are really games for children, where they play at jumping over one another or moving within a circle to the rhythm of the music. But because dances have such meaning to the Africans, children also learn the expected behavior for their particular tribe. For them, wearing masks or celebration clothing while they dance not only involves a handing down of tradition but it prepares them for membership in the adult societies.

JIVE, AN AMERICAN DANCE WITH AFRICAN ROOTS

African American slaves were the first to dance what is known today as "jive." These slaves danced several native dances that had triple and single steps. Their music had a continuous drum bass, and several hints of jive rhythms. Jive today has split into two parts, one based on this original African beat and the other based upon its evolved style. Jive is sometimes called Swing, the Jitterbug, the Lindyhop, or the Charleston, although jive is actually a different dance from all of these. These dances are all similar, however, and their steps are interconnected. The music for jive is in 4/4 time, which means four beats to a measure, the quarter note being the dominant note of the measure. It is done with a series of single and triple steps.

During times of celebration and times of every day living, dance helps define many parts of the social structure within a tribe. It also provides individuals with the role they need to feel instrumental in their particular society. Dance serves an important purpose for the African people.

The Africans who came to North America as slaves brought this heritage of dance with them. Far from the land where it was born, it continued to shape and influence the dance traditions of African Americans.

The hand-clapping and repetitive movements that were common in Africa were also trademarks of African American dance. One African American dance, called "Ball the Jack," featured "snake hips"—wavelike hip motions while the feet and head remained still. The name of this dance comes from the verse that the dancers recite: "And I ball the jack on the railroad track." This referred to the railroad signal for proceeding full speed ahead. For African American slaves, trains and the railroad were symbols for escape and freedom—and the dance and its words urged African Americans to be fast and brave as they fled to freedom in the North. Dance traditions like these, rooted both in Africa and the New World, offered captive African Americans hope and courage.

Chinese dancers often wear elaborate costumes.

EIGHT

Asian Folk Dances
Concentration and Poise

A Thai dancer demonstrates her cultural pride.

IN A SMALL VILLAGE in Japan there lived a man and woman who had no children. They prayed that the gods would give them a child, even if he were only as small as a thumb.

Their prayer was answered and they had a son. He was only the size of a thumb and he never grew any taller. But his parents loved him and named him Issun Boshi. Their little son delighted them. He was especially good at dancing.

When he was older, there were monsters in the capital that would catch small girls. Issun Boshi told his parents that he wanted to go to the capital to drive away the monsters so that the people would no longer be worried and scared. His parents only laughed, knowing that Issun Boshi was far too little to do any good against the monsters. But they wanted their son to be happy, so they sent him to live with a master in the city.

At his master's house, Issun Boshi would dance on the master's palm. The guests enjoyed this entertainment greatly and he became very famous. The master's daughter also liked Issun Boshi very much, and they enjoyed dancing and playing together.

The girl wanted to go to the temple to pray, so the master sent many strong men with her to protect her from the monsters. Issun Boshi hid in her sleeves.

On the way home from the temple, two monsters attacked the princess. The strong men tried to defend her, but the monsters were too strong. But just as the monsters were about to grab the princess, Issun Boshi pulled out his sword.

The monster laughed, picked him up, and swallowed him.

Folk dancers from Laos.

But Issun Boshi danced inside the monster's stomach, waving his needle sword around his head so that it pierced the monster's stomach and he had to spit out Issun Boshi. The other monster tried to catch him—but Issun Boshi danced and waved his needle, piercing the monster's eyes.

Only when the monsters had fled, did Issun Boshi stop dancing. As the master's daughter thanked him for his help, she noticed something on the ground. "It looks like the monster left a treasure hammer. You can wish for anything with it."

"Please shake it for me and wish that I would grow taller," Issun Boshi said.

As soon as the girl made the wish, Issun Boshi grew into a tall, good-looking man. He and the master's daughter married and everyone came to dance with them at their marriage.

One may judge a king by the state of dancing during his reign.

—*Chinese proverb*

He who cannot dance puts the blame on the floor.

—*Hindu proverb*

Over 400 *mudras* (gestures) are a part of India's classical dance. The dancer is able to share complex ideas, emotions, and relationships. Because the mudras are a part everyday life in India, those watching the performances inderstand the story being related.

He became a wise government official, and his parents lived with them happily ever after.

IN this Japanese folktale, dancing is the means by which Issun Boshi overcomes his small size. His dancing ability gains him popularity, fierce courage, and good luck.

In Japan, both old and young celebrate by dancing. Their traditional dances are very controlled; all of their movements hold meaning for the dancers and the audience. Young children learn these dances that also teach them what is expected as behavior from them.

Japan's folk dances are called *odori*. One kind of odori, the *bon* dance, is one that offers welcome to the spirits of the dead. The Japanese people believe these spirits visit the living, and through singing and dancing they make the spirits feel welcome. The circle dance moves slowly, then quickly, then slowly again.

Celebrating the harvest is a dancing rite repeated from country to country. The Hounen-Odori is the Japanese version of the harvest festival. It is celebrated in August, on the 15th day of the harvest moon. Because of the bright full moon, the people are able to harvest at night. They offer thanks to the sun, water, and earth for yielding a good crop, such as wheat, barley, and rice. The festivities include traditional Japanese dance, music, kimonos (traditional dress), and foods. Although Japanese immigrants to North America may no longer participate in harvesting, they still celebrate with their traditional dances.

Immigrants from Indonesia bring

The Japanese Lion Dance tells a story.

Tal is a series of musical beats that provides a framework to the Indian dance *kathak*. Dancers improvise intricate steps as they dance, which can be difficult unless the dancers are well trained.

their own dance traditions to the United States and Canada. In Bali, dance is considered a learning process. Everyone is free to watch lessons as children learn through imitation. By placing a child's limbs in the correct positions, relatives begin teaching children sometimes before they can walk.

These children learn to wear a tranquil, mask-like face. Their arms are held at sharp angles, the torso is straight with a slightly arched spine, and they perform barefoot.

Chinese Americans have brought yet another dance heritage to North America. The dragon is a popular figure in Chinese folk dance, and the dragon dance was originally done to expel devils and evil spirits and to bring good luck to the people. Today, the dragon is made into a costume that is then worn by several dancers who are proud to represent this beast of nobility.

According to Chinese legend, a long time ago a strange dragon-like creature appeared in China. Because he ate men and animals, they were

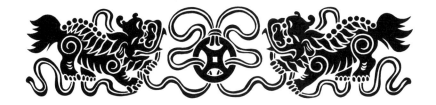

very scared of him. He was very fast and extremely fierce; the people called him Nien, which in Chinese sounds like the word for "year."

No one could fight Nien, not even the fox or the tiger. So the people went to the lion to ask him to save them. The lion attacked the creature and wounded it. But as he left, Nien announced he would return to get revenge on the people.

In the meantime the lion guarded the emperor's gate. One year later, when Nien returned, the lion could not help them, so the villagers decided to fight Nien themselves. They made an image of the lion out of bamboo and cloth. Two men wore the costume as they approached the dragon monster. The men pranced and roared and scared the creature away again.

This is the reason why there is the lion dance every year on the eve of the Chinese New Year. Participants are frightening evil away for another year. Two male dancers wear the lion's costume. Three musicians, playing a large drum, cymbals, and a gong, join the lion dancers, who are experts in kung fu. The musicians follow the moves of the dancers as they move along enacting the story of the lion. The dragon dance is often a part of Chinese New Year's celebrations across North America.

Many Asian dances are performed for healing the sick. For instance, a medicine man from the Sarawak tribe of Malaysia may dance a frenzied appeal to rid the person of evil spirits. He even uses a sword in a battle

> The Marquesan girls dance all over; not only do their feet dance, but their arms, hands, fingers, aye, their very eyes seem to dance in their heads.
>
> —*Herman Melville*

Many Asian dances involve large numbers of dancers in intricate movements that tell a story.

Around the world, religious beliefs and experiences strongly influence dance. Many of Korea's folk dances, for example, combine dance with drama, act out stories with spiritual messages. The traditional masked dance plays feature demon masks, medicine masks, and spirit masks. Animal masks were once worn to keep wild animals appeased. The masks were thought to hold magic even after the dance was complete.

Korean dance outfits often add to the beauty and message of the dance. In some traditional dances, large, intricately decorated fans work to extend the movements of the participants. When viewed from the audience, they provide color and shape that could not be achieved without such stunning props.

Dancers from Bali.

against the spirits causing the illness. Another dance of Sarawak is performed to help women when they are giving birth. Some of these healing dance traditions have made their way to North America as well.

In Sri Lanka, devil dancing is performed for illnesses or pregnancy; this form of dance is also used during adversities or to prevent tragedies. A special shrine is built outside, and the dancers, all male, dress as women with red clothes on their heads and bells on their ankles. The dance is long and includes leaping and swirling; it ends when the dancers put on masks and make the demon explain itself so that the sick person can recover.

In India, folk dance is widespread and diverse. Traditionally, the **caste system** placed each person into a social standing from which they could never depart, and folk dances carried with them the structures of the society. For example, the *kolyacha* is a fisherman's dance from the west central region of India.

> Religions like Buddhism and Hinduism dance as a form of worship. In fact, some religious statues depict figures dancing.

A Japanese dancer.

A dancer from Java.

Cambodian dancers move slowly in smooth wavelike steps. They wear comfortable clothes while they practice flexibility. But when these highly trained artists perform for audiences, seamstresses actually sew them into their costumes. Practicing for the movements is a very important part of their training. Repeating specific exercises allows dancers' fingers and elbows to become so supple that they appear to be without bones.

The men dance as if rowing a boat, moving with sliding steps. The women, their partners, wave handkerchiefs to encourage their efforts.

Weddings are a time of prolific dancing in India. The *kolis* dance consists of moving through the streets with pots, pans, and other kitchen necessities as gifts for the newly married couple. In another marriage dance, men dress like a bridegroom, with a beautiful papier-maché horse built on bamboo covering the lower parts of their bodies. These *kacchi ghori* dancers then perform a joust. The riders carry shields and long swords for their dance contests.

Masks are popular with dancers from India and Tibet. The yak dance features a dancer who dresses to look like a yak and then performs with another man on his back. Grinning wooden masks, representing the spirits of the other world, contrast with silk and brocade long tunics worn by the *sada topo tsen* dancers. The men dance with powerful, slow twirling and hopping movements.

Sri Lankan dancers.

A folk dancer from Bali.

No, a Japanese dance, is a form of drama. It is very slow moving and uses gestures, breathing, and music to show the idea of opposing forces. These performances are slow and very long.

The elaborate facial make-up and stiff faces of other dancers add dimension and meaning to the folk dance. Whether trying to appease a deity with the praise of dance and song, offering a sacrifice during a dance, or dancing to keep away an epidemic, the Indian culture is affected by the steps and the meaning behind these long-standing traditions.

Many Asian folk dances require great concentration and poise. The movements are pre-

A community dance in Fiji.

cise and carried out with much feeling, many times even in a trance-like state. From healings to celebrations, dance brings meaning and hope to the people who perform them. These ancient dance traditions from Asia have become a part of North America's mosaic of cultural traditions.

Further Reading

Grau, Andree. *Eyewitness Books Dance.* New York: Alfred A. Knopf, 1998.

Greene, Hank. *Square and Folk Dancing.* New York: Harper & Row, 1984.

Kraus, Richard. *History of the Dance.* Englewood Cliffs, N.J.: Prentice-Hall, 1999.

Nevell, Richard. *A Time to Dance.* New York: St. Martin's, 1997.

Tythacott, Louise. *Traditions Around the World of Dance.* New York: Thomson Learning, 1995.

More Information

iety

lifornia
k_dance_federation_of_california.html

www.folkdancing.org

National Dance Institute
594 Broadway, Room 805
New York, NY 10012
202-226-0083

National Square Dance Directory
Box 880
Brandon, MS 39043

San Francisco Ethnic Dance Festival
Fort Mason Center
Landmark Building D
San Francisco, CA 94123

Swing Street.com
www.streetswing.com/homepage.htm

Glossary

Caste system   Hereditary social classifications that restrict the occupations and interactions of their members.

Fiesta   A Spanish party or celebration.

Icons   Religious pictures with symbolic meaning.

Intermediary   A person who acts as a go-between.

Itinerant   Traveling.

Lent   The period of preparation before Easter.

Mariachi   A Mexican street band.

Metaphor   A symbol; a comparison between two things that increases our understanding.

Mumming   Performing in disguise, often going from house to house, during festivals.

Nomads   People without any settled home who travel from place to place.

Pantomime   To act out with physical motions and no words.

Parody   A silly or ridiculous imitation.

Percussion   Having to do with beating or striking.

Pirouetting   Turning, spinning.

Promenade   A ceremonial grand march of all the dancers.

Secular   Relating to worldly concerns rather than religious.

Theology   The study of God and one's relationship to him.

Index

Biographies

Sherry Bonnice lives in a log cabin on a dirt road in Montrose, Pennsylvania, with her husband, teenage daughter, five dogs, and 25 rabbits. She loves homeschooling her daughter, reading, and making quilts. Sherry has spent the last two years coediting three quilt magazines and writing a quilt book. Writing books for children and young people has been her dream.

Dr. Alan Jabbour is a folklorist who served as the founding director of the American Folklife Center at the Library of Congress from 1976 to 1999. Previously, he began the grant-giving program in folk arts at the National Endowment for the Arts (1974–1976). A native of Jacksonville, Florida, he was trained at the University of Miami (B.A.) and Duke University (M.A., Ph.D.). A violinist from childhood on, he documented old-time fiddling in the Upper South in the 1960s and 1970s. A specialist in instrumental folk music, he is known as a fiddler himself, an art he acquired directly from elderly fiddlers in North Carolina, Virginia, and West Virginia. He has taught folklore and folk music at UCLA and the University of Maryland and has published widely in the field.